SCIENCE MASTERS

EARTH'S ENERGY FLOW

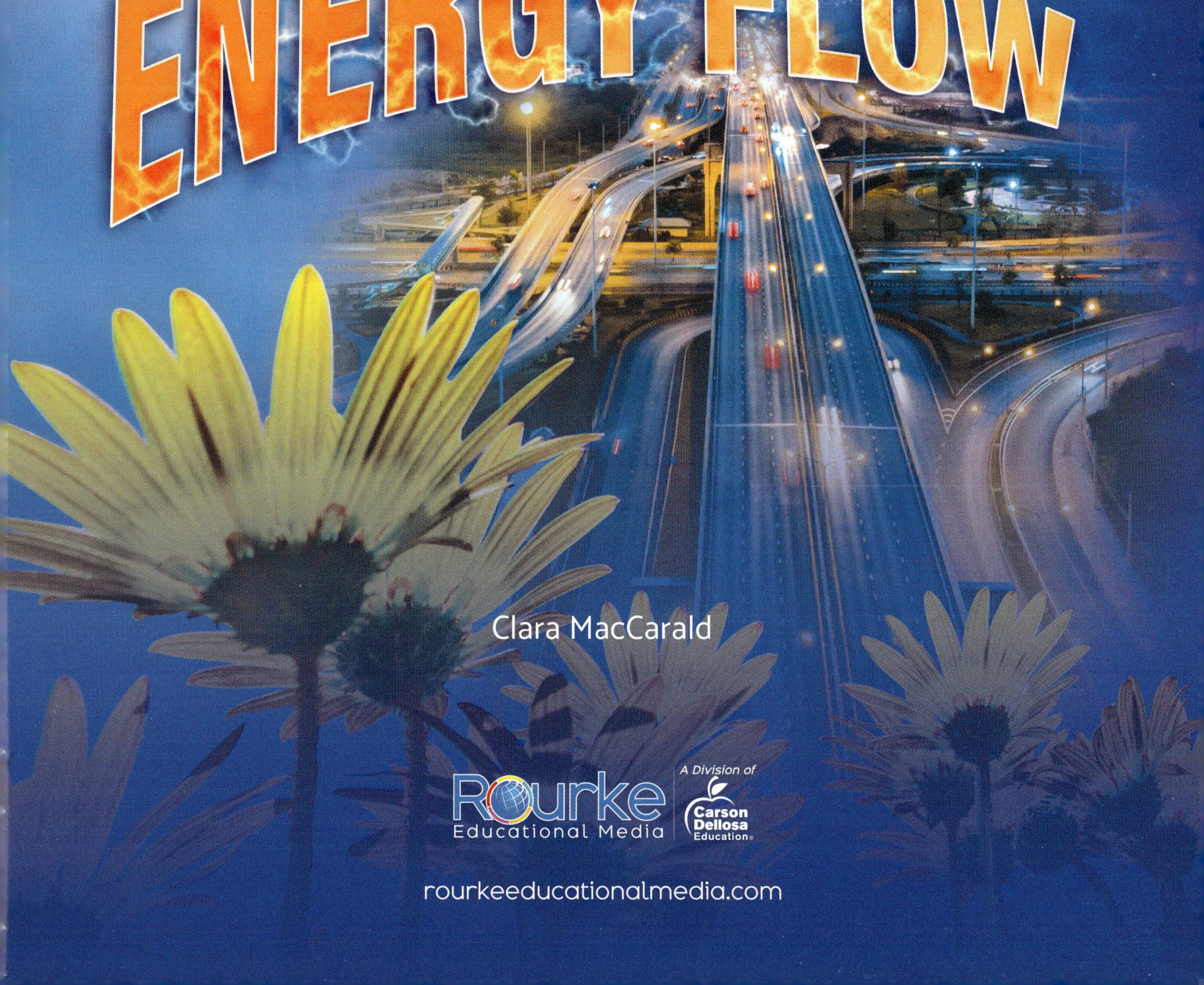

Clara MacCarald

Rourke Educational Media
A Division of Carson Dellosa Education
rourkeeducationalmedia.com

ROURKE'S

SCHOOL to HOME

CONNECTIONS

BEFORE AND DURING READING ACTIVITIES

Before Reading: *Building Background Knowledge and Vocabulary*

Building background knowledge can help children process new information and build upon what they already know. Before reading a book, it is important to tap into what children already know about the topic. This will help them develop their vocabulary and increase their reading comprehension.

Questions and Activities to Build Background Knowledge:

1. Look at the front cover of the book and read the title. What do you think this book will be about?
2. What do you already know about this topic?
3. Take a book walk and skim the pages. Look at the table of contents, photographs, captions, and bold words. Did these text features give you any information or predictions about what you will read in this book?

Vocabulary: *Vocabulary Is Key to Reading Comprehension*

Use the following directions to prompt a conversation about each word.

- Read the vocabulary words.
- What comes to mind when you see each word?
- What do you think each word means?

Vocabulary Words:

- *absorbed*
- *air pressure*
- *alternatives*
- *atmosphere*
- *consumers*
- *droughts*
- *feedback*
- *friction*
- *fuels*
- *fungi*
- *magma*
- *matter*

During Reading: *Reading for Meaning and Understanding*

To achieve deep comprehension of a book, children are encouraged to use close reading strategies. During reading, it is important to have children stop and make connections. These connections result in deeper analysis and understanding of a book.

Close Reading a Text

During reading, have children stop and talk about the following:

- Any confusing parts
- Any unknown words
- Text to text, text to self, text to world connections
- The main idea in each chapter or heading

Encourage children to use context clues to determine the meaning of any unknown words. These strategies will help children learn to analyze the text more thoroughly as they read.

When you are finished reading this book, turn to the next-to-last page for **Text-Dependent Questions** and an **Extension Activity**.

TABLE OF CONTENTS

CHAPTER ONE

ENERGY ON EARTH

Sometimes adults tell young people they have too much energy. What is energy? What does it do and where does it come from? Energy is defined as the ability to do work. In this case, *work* doesn't mean the tasks people do at a job. It means moving or changing **matter**.

Movement—by flying, walking, or other means—takes lots of energy.

Energy is everywhere you look. All living things use energy to live and grow. Energy is in the food you eat. It's in your muscles as you work and play. Energy is found in the sky as sunshine or wind. Gravity has energy. Flowing rivers and waterfalls have energy. Vehicles run using the energy stored in **fuels**, which often come from deep underground.

Some kinds of energy are easy to see because they involve things moving about. Other kinds of energy are easy to overlook. Energy can come in the form of heat, like from a stove. It can come in the form of light, like from a lightbulb. Some energy is stored. The stored energy must be released before it can do work. For example, the calories found in food just sit there until your body uses them as a source of fuel.

Applying your energy to wheels can help you go farther and faster.

James Prescott Joule
1818–1889

What Is a Joule?

James Prescott Joule was an English physicist. He experimented with creating heat by moving paddles in water and by running electricity through wires. His work led him to realize that all forms of energy can be changed into each other. A joule *is now the name for a unit of energy.*

It's not only stored energy that changes into different forms. Energy doesn't like to sit still. You can convert one kind of energy into another by rubbing your hands together and feeling how your skin warms.

The harder you rub your hands together, the more heat gets produced.

The movement of your hands creates **friction**, which turns motion energy into heat energy. An engine burns gasoline, turning stored energy into heat energy, which the engine then turns into motion.

Burning fuel makes hot gases expand in a car's engine. The gases make the engine parts move, which then turn the wheels.

Although energy can change, it can't disappear. Earth has an energy budget that accounts for all the energy found on the planet. Energy enters the **atmosphere**, mostly from the sun, and energy eventually goes out into space. In between, energy warms Earth's ecosystems and powers its food webs.

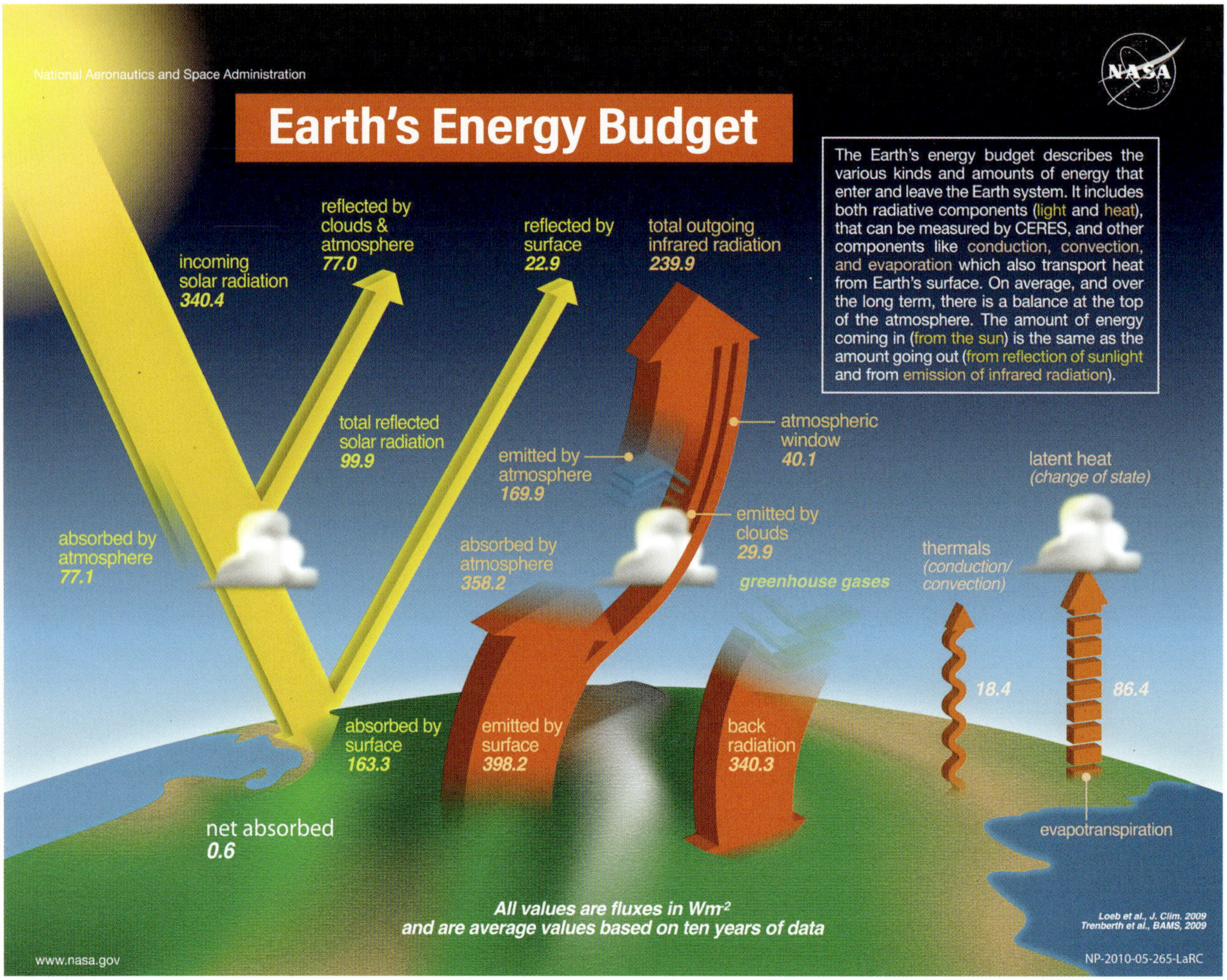

About a third of the sun's energy is reflected away from Earth. The rest becomes a part of the energy cycle.

Law of Conservation of Energy

The law of conservation of energy is not a government law to save fuel. It's a basic law of physics: Energy cannot be created or destroyed. It can only be changed. On Earth, that means that all the energy coming into the atmosphere must go somewhere, even if only out to space.

CHAPTER TWO

THE POWER OF THE SUN

Life on Earth exists because of the greenhouse effect. During the day, the sun shines on Earth. Some energy is **absorbed** by the atmosphere and the surface while the rest is reflected. At night, the surface of Earth gives off some of the energy it holds. If Earth lost all of this energy to space, Earth would be too cold to support life as we know it.

The greenhouse effect allows Earth's atmosphere to trap much of the sun's energy.

The air outside a greenhouse can be cold...

Luckily, the atmosphere contains greenhouse gases that absorb heat and keep our planet toasty. The glass of a greenhouse does something similar by trapping heat, which would otherwise be lost to the air.

...but inside, it can be 20 degrees Fahrenheit (11 degrees Celsius) warmer.

The Sun's Rays and Earth

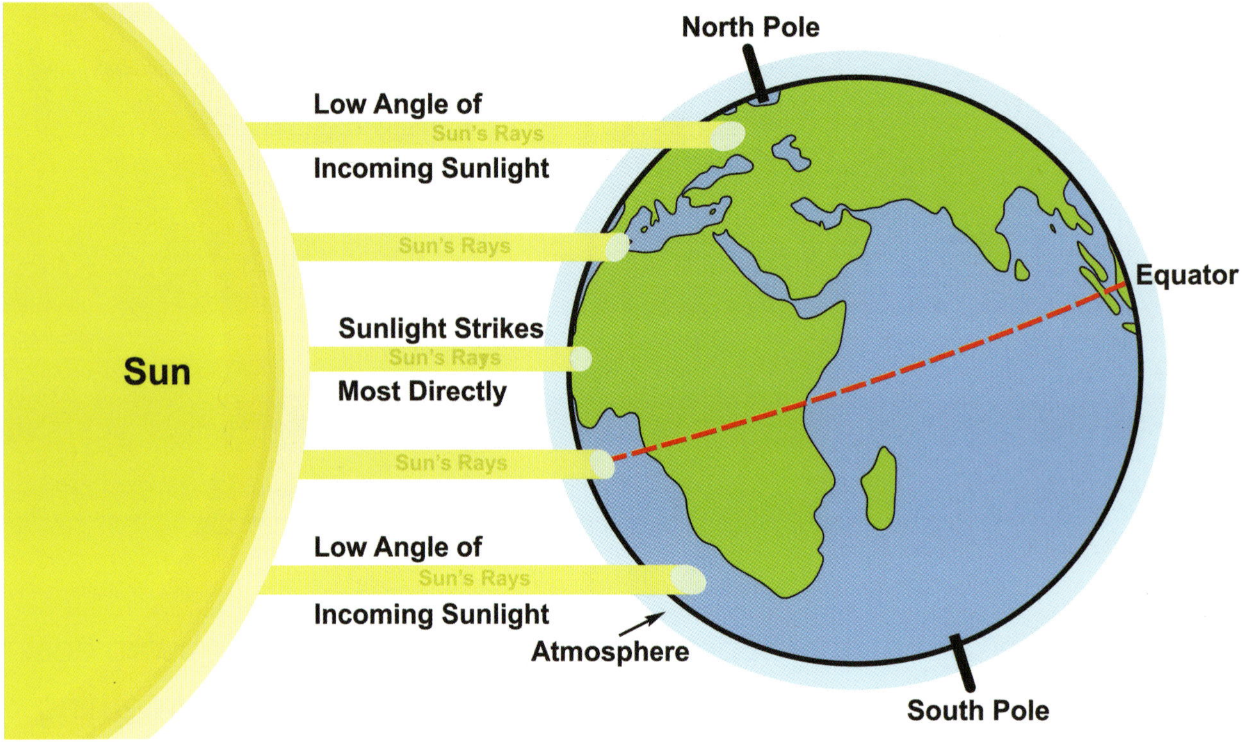

The angle of sunlight as it hits Earth depends on both the latitude and the time of year.

Not all parts of Earth receive or absorb the same amount of energy. For one thing, Earth is a globe. The sun's rays pack more energy when they hit something straight-on rather than at an angle. So, Earth receives more energy near the equator than it does near the two poles.

Earth also spins on an axis tilted 23.5 degrees. This tilt causes the seasons. On the first day of summer in the North, the North Pole tilts 23.5 degrees toward the sun. On the first day of the northern winter, the North Pole tilts the same angle away from the sun.

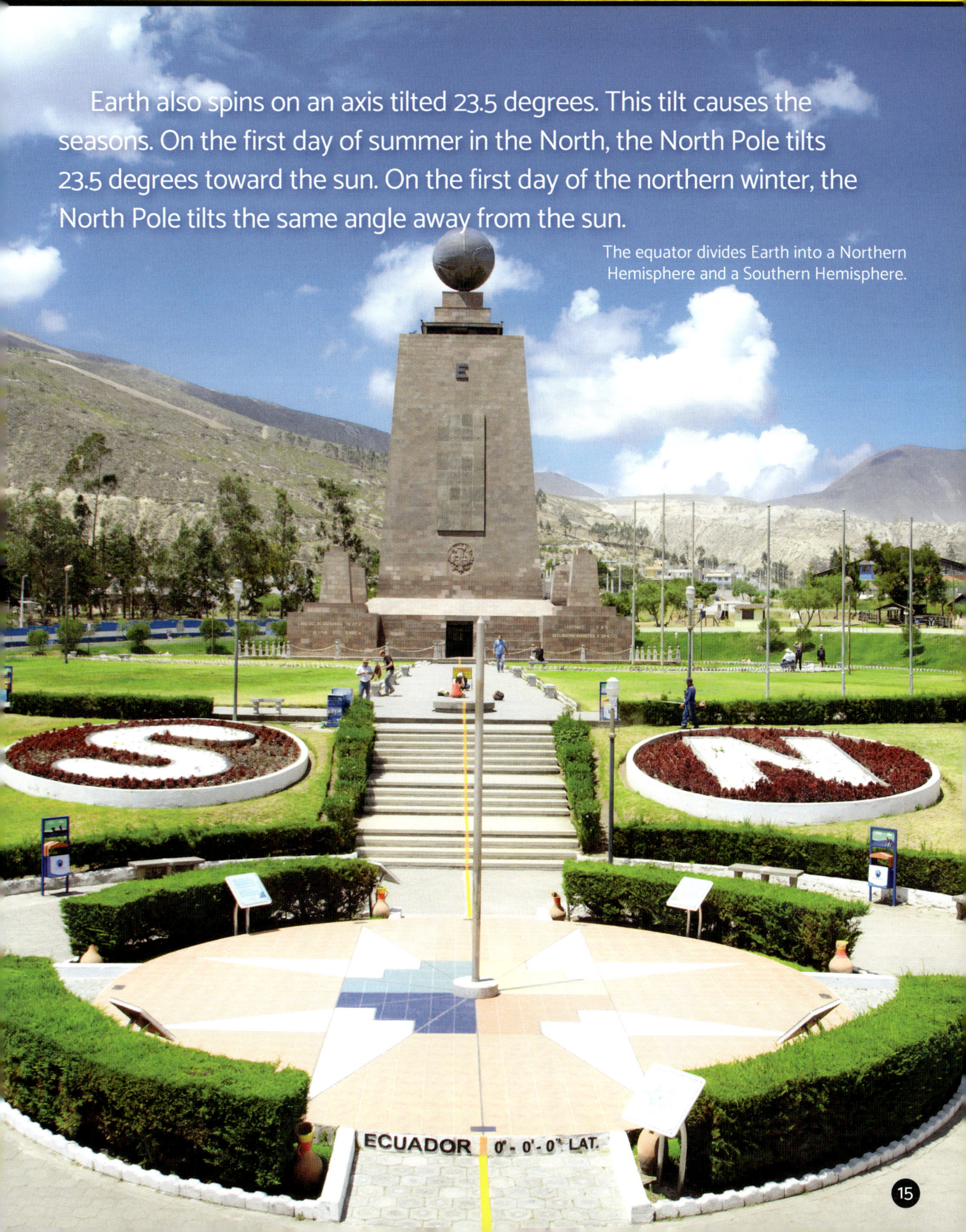

The equator divides Earth into a Northern Hemisphere and a Southern Hemisphere.

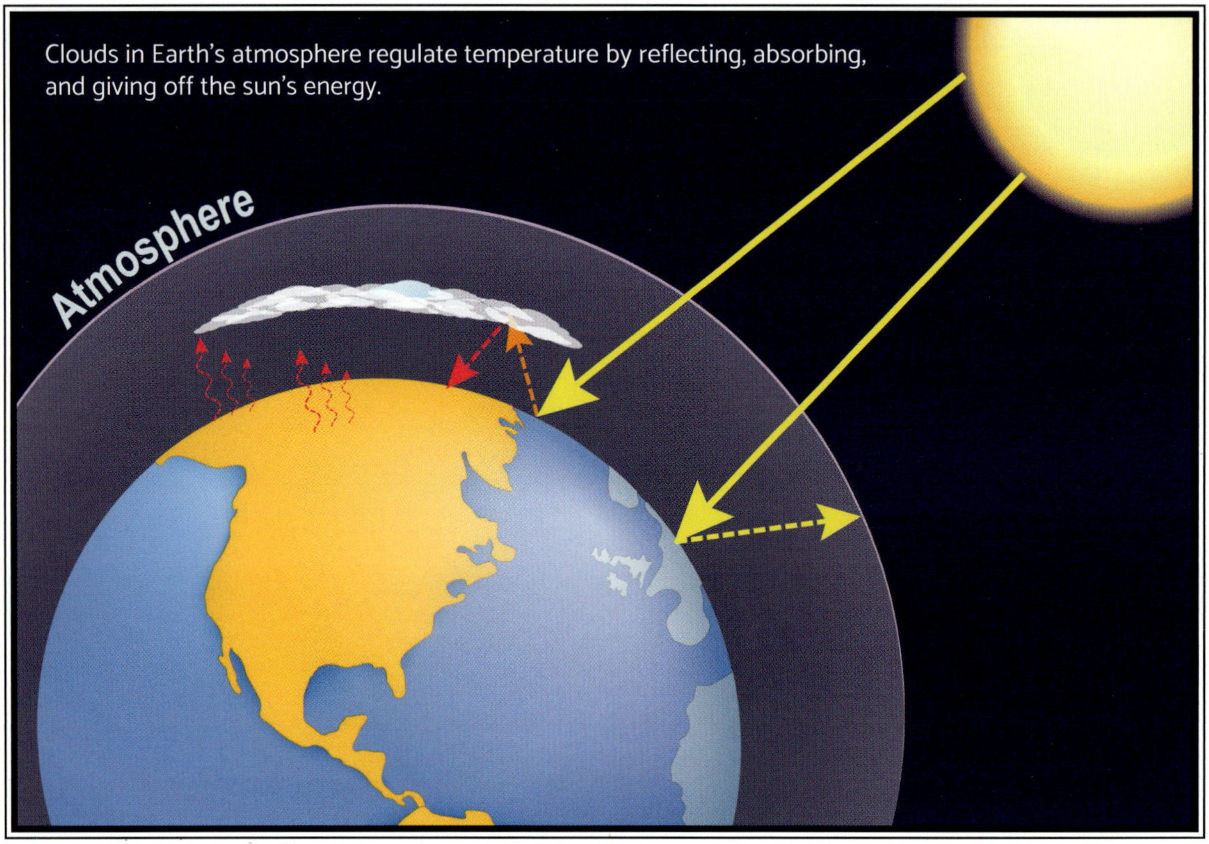

Clouds in Earth's atmosphere regulate temperature by reflecting, absorbing, and giving off the sun's energy.

Features of Earth's atmosphere and surface also change how much sun energy is absorbed, reflected, or given off. Clouds can reflect sunlight during the day. They can also trap heat given off by Earth. Bright surfaces, such as snow, reflect more energy than dark surfaces, such as roadways and buildings.

Hotter areas are shown in red. Cooler areas are shown in blue.

A thermal imaging camera translates heat into visible light.

Hot Cities

Cities can be several degrees warmer than the areas surrounding them. Roads and buildings absorb more heat than trees and grass. Tall buildings can also trap heat and keep the wind from blowing it away. Add vehicles, factories, and other heat producers and you end up with an urban heat island.

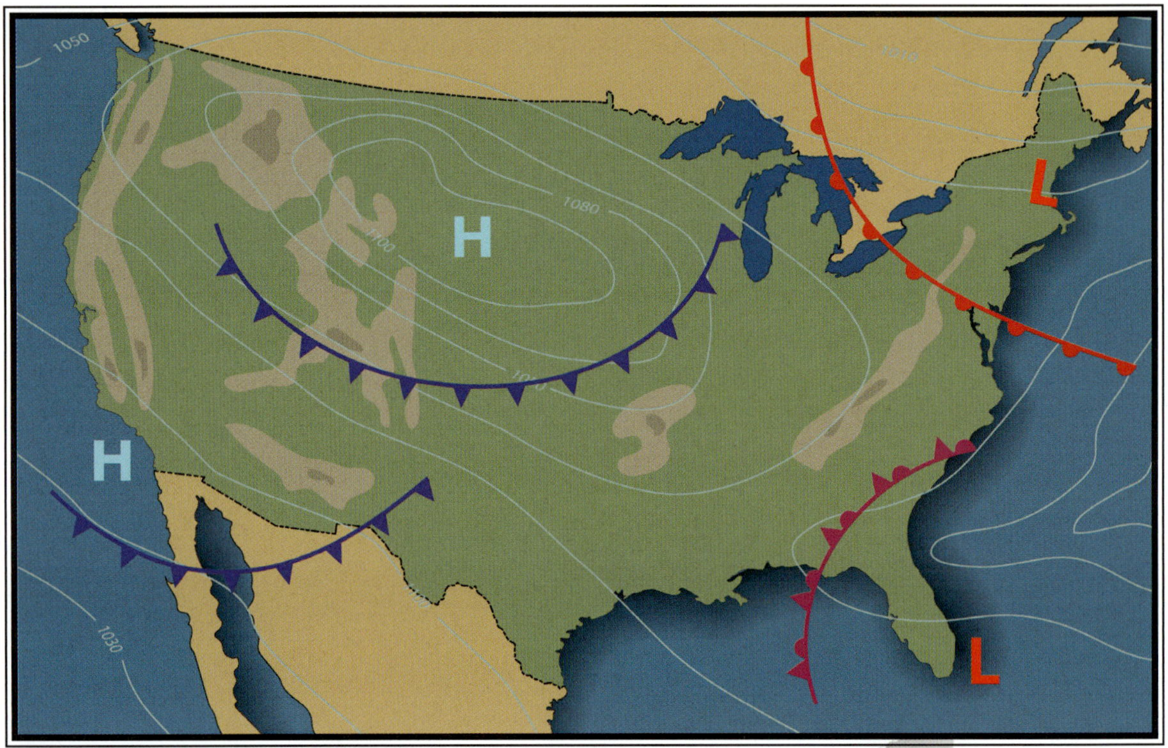

Weather maps show areas of high (H) and low (L) air pressure.

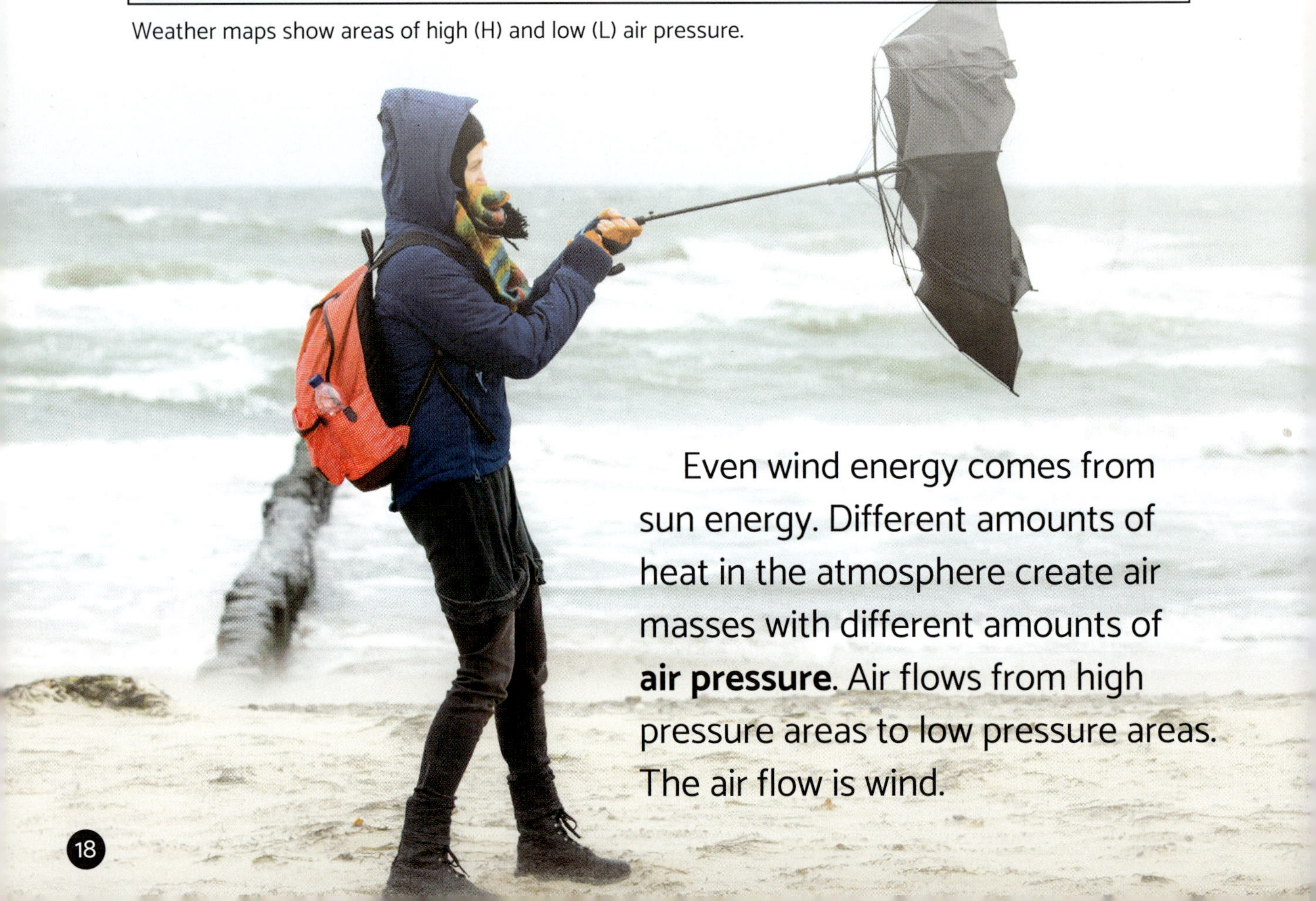

Even wind energy comes from sun energy. Different amounts of heat in the atmosphere create air masses with different amounts of **air pressure**. Air flows from high pressure areas to low pressure areas. The air flow is wind.

Most energy on Earth comes from the sun, but not all. Some wind energy comes from Earth's spin. Some energy comes from below Earth's crust. **Magma** has enormous amounts of heat energy. This energy can warm the surface at hot springs or erupt from volcanoes. Still more energy comes from Earth's gravity. It does work by making water flow downhill and objects roll down slopes. The moon's gravity is part of what produces Earth's tides.

Tidal Energy

Tidal energy in the ocean comes from the moon's gravity, the sun's gravity, and Earth's spin. Most of the ocean has two high tides each day. The highest tides happen when the moon and sun line up. People have invented machines that can harness power from the tides.

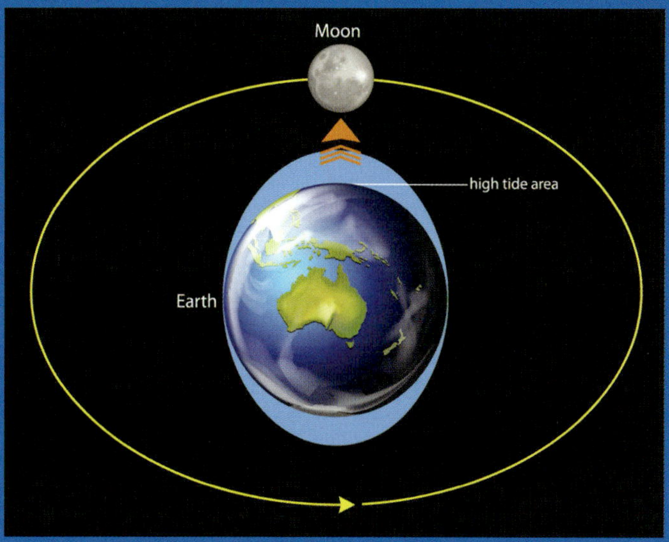

CHAPTER THREE

ENERGY WEBS

Animals must find food, escape from predators, and raise their young. To do all this, they need a lot of energy. Like you, animals get the energy they need from the food they eat. Food contains stored energy. Where does the energy in food come from? It can all be traced back to the sun.

Each wolf in a pack must get enough energy to survive.

Every food chain begins with a producer. Producers are organisms that make their own food. Almost all producers do this by absorbing energy from the sun and storing it in organic compounds through a process called *photosynthesis*. Producers include plants, algae, and some kinds of bacteria. The producers you eat—fruits, vegetables, and grains—contain stored sun energy.

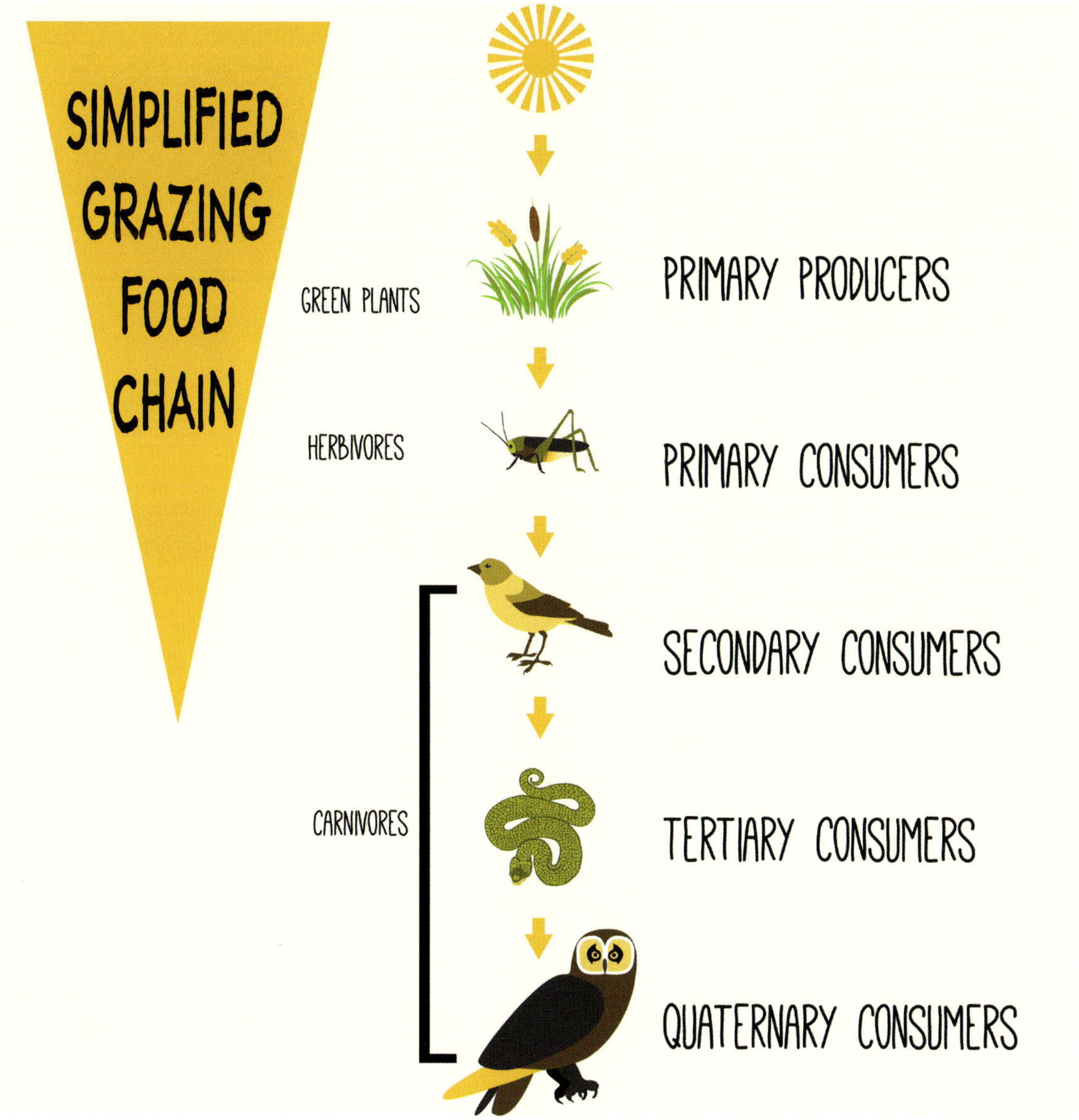

In addition to producers, food chains contain **consumers**. Consumers cannot use energy from sunlight to make food. They must eat producers or other consumers, which their bodies break down into organic compounds. The cells of consumers release the energy stored in these organic compounds to move, grow, and stay warm.

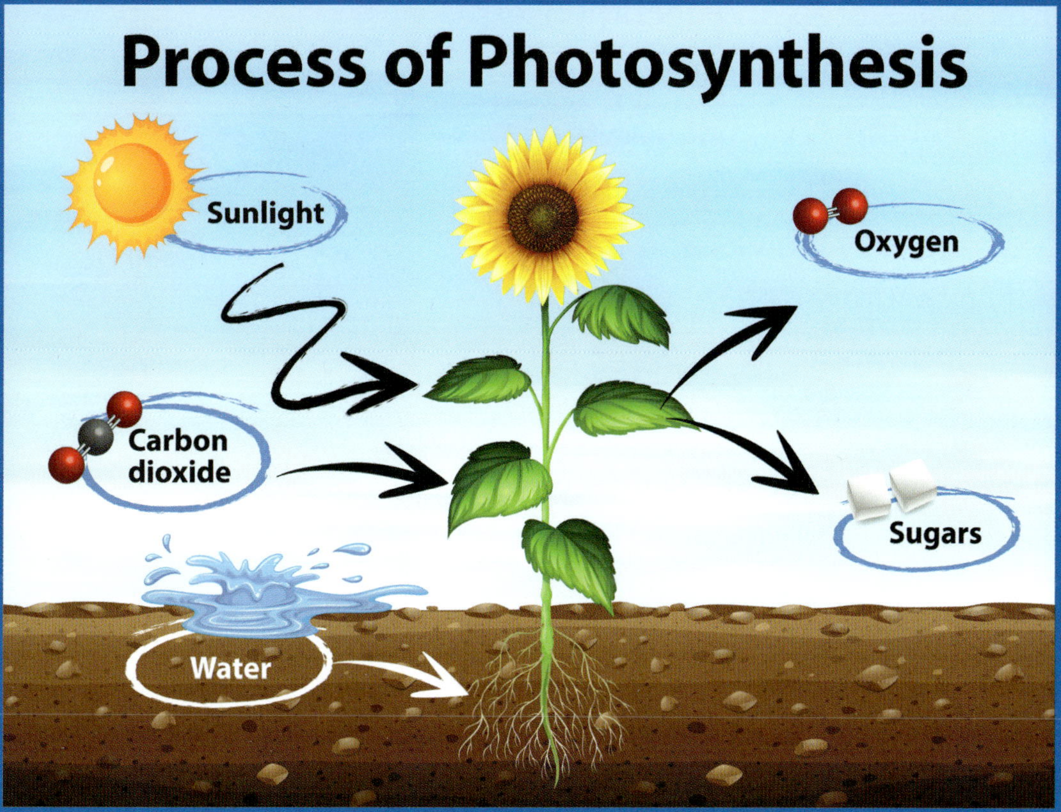

Photosynthesis

Organisms that perform photosynthesis contain pigments that capture light energy. They use the energy to break apart molecules of water from the soil and molecules of carbon dioxide from the air. The plant combines the pieces to make oxygen and sugar, a powerful food. Pigments commonly used for photosynthesis are green, but others are red, orange, or yellow.

Consumers include herbivores, carnivores, omnivores, and decomposers. Herbivores, such as white-tailed deer and aphids, eat material that comes from producers, such as leaves and sap. Carnivores like gray wolves and lions eat mostly consumers, such as white-tailed deer and zebras. Omnivores eat both producers and consumers. Black bears are omnivores. They eat a variety of foods including fruit, nuts, fish, and sometimes fawns. Humans are also omnivores, though some choose not to eat meat.

Carnivores spend a lot of energy hunting. Their prey must replenish that lost energy and provide more. If chasing a rabbit and chasing a deer take the same amount of energy, carnivores will choose the deer!

Salmon are high in calories, providing lots of energy for bears.

A Balanced Diet

Few animals eat only producers or only consumers without ever straying from their diets. For example, wolves like to snack on fruit. Deer will gnaw on animal carcasses and snatch chicks out of bird nests. The deer eat animals for their minerals rather than as a major source of energy.

Worms are decomposers. Their waste, called *castings*, is full of nutrients for plants.

Mushrooms, a type of fungi, and other decomposers release carbon, nitrogen, and other nutrients back into the soil.

Decomposers are a special kind of consumer. Decomposers such as **fungi** break down dead organisms or animal waste in order to release energy.

A food web is all the food chains in one environment. Each step in a food web has less energy than the step before it. This is because each organism uses some energy and loses some as heat, which means that less energy is available at each new connection in the food web.

Decomposers can recycle matter by breaking it down into forms that can be used by plants. Energy, however, flows only one way through the food web. When it's gone, it's gone. Producers must absorb new energy to make more food.

Deep-Sea Vents

At deep-sea vents, food webs are powered by magma inside Earth. Openings in the rocks release heat and chemicals into the ocean. Bacteria that gather around the vents use these chemicals as a source of energy. Other organisms consume the bacteria as food.

CHAPTER FOUR

FUELING THE WORLD

All animals need energy. But humans have invented more ways to use energy than any other creature. Look around you. Lights, heating equipment, electronic devices, kitchen appliances, and vehicles all require energy to work. Where does this energy come from? Most of it originally came from the sun.

Before humans learned to start fires themselves, they may have gathered fires started by lightning.

Prehistoric humans understood how to burn wood and other plant material in a controlled way. The energy released by their fires was the same energy the plants had captured from the sun. For a long time, people used fires to cook food, to keep warm, and to melt and use other materials such as metal.

More than a thousand years ago, people discovered substances from within Earth that burned even better: fossil fuels. Fossil fuels include coal, oil, and natural gas. People began to widely use fossil fuels in the mid-1700s to power the Industrial Revolution.

Long before the Industrial Revolution, coal was used by the ancient Chinese, the Romans, and the Hopi people.

Oil wells bore deep in the Earth to find fossil fuels.

Evolving Planet

The Industrial Revolution marked a rapid change from agricultural societies to machine-driven societies. Tools, clothing, and other items made by factories and mass-production replaced handmade items. New inventions and new power sources changed the way people lived, worked, and traveled. But burning fossil fuels for power created a new source of air and water pollution. The air in growing cities became smoggy. The concentration of carbon dioxide in Earth's atmosphere increased.

OIL AND GAS RESOURCES

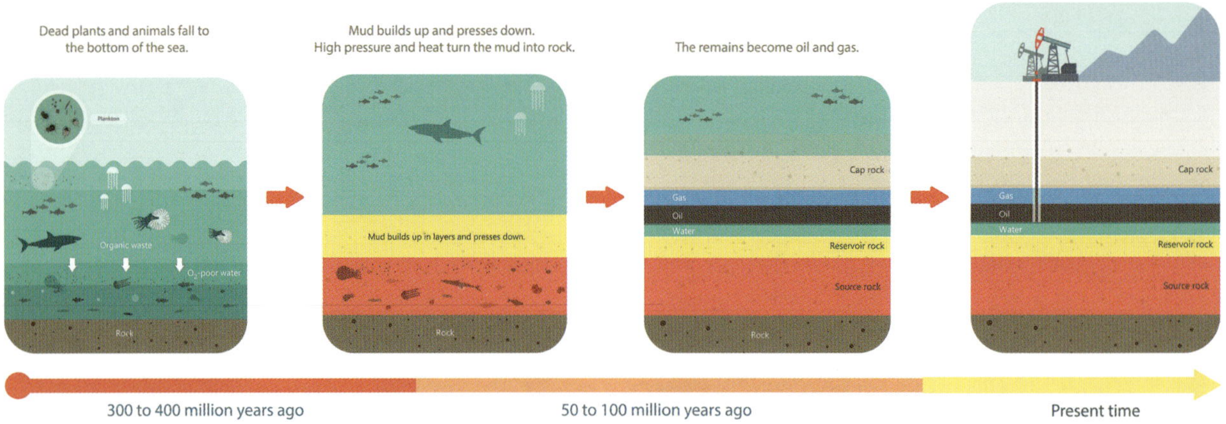

Fossil fuels have an ancient origin. Originally, their energy came from the sun. Over millions of years, some plants and animals became buried rather than being eaten or fully decomposed. Over time, the land rose, burying the organic material even deeper. Pressure from above and extreme heat from deep inside Earth converted the organic material into fossil fuels.

Drilling rigs excavate coal from mines deep underground.

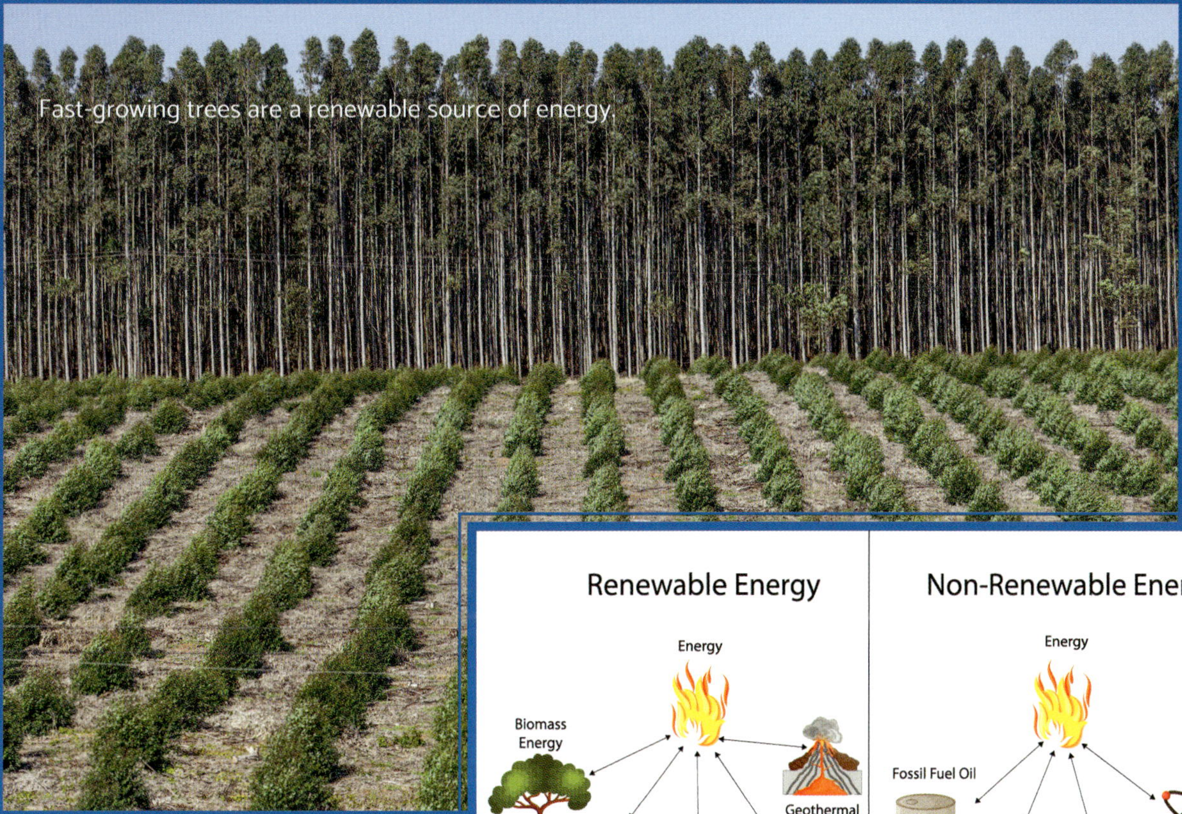

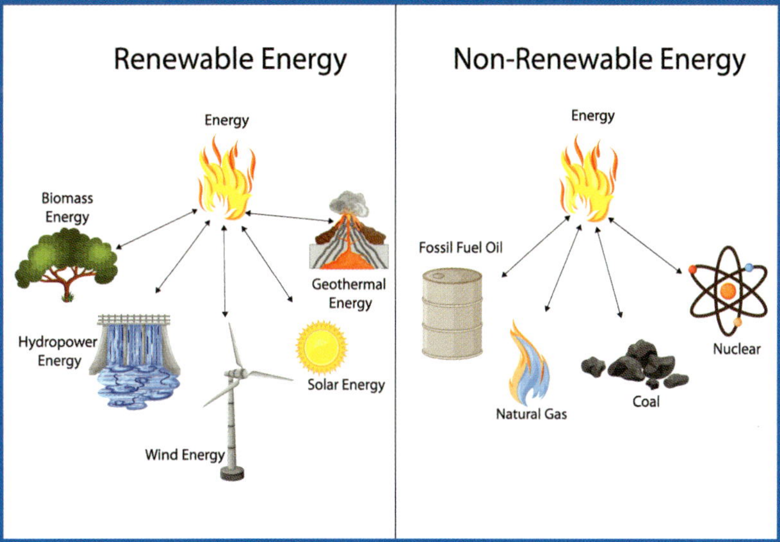

Non-Renewable or Renewable?

Renewable resources are created by natural processes faster than people use them up. Fossil fuels are non-renewable resources because they take a long time to form. New solar and wind power arrives every day. They are renewable resources. Wood can be renewable if it grows faster than it is harvested.

New technologies can reduce pollution released by burning fossil fuels, but industries complain about the costs.

Power plants burn fossil fuels to produce electricity. Many vehicles burn fossil fuels. Unfortunately, when fossil fuels are burned, they release pollution as well as energy. Some pollution dirties the air and threatens the health of people and animals. Burning fossil fuels also increases the amount of greenhouse gases in the atmosphere.

Wind farms produce clean, renewable energy.

Humans have invented many **alternatives** to fossil fuels. Solar panels capture sunlight and turn it into a source of electric power. Wind power comes from the sun and Earth. Geothermal energy comes from heat found under Earth's crust. While some ancient people used the geothermal energy found at hot springs, modern technology lets people drill down deep and convert geothermal energy into electricity.

On solar farms, the angle of panels can be changed to capture the sun's rays.

Edmond Becquerel
1820–1891

Sun Electricity

In 1839, French physicist Edmond Becquerel discovered how to produce electricity using sunlight. Inventors tried different methods over the years but couldn't capture much power. Finally, in 1954, U.S. inventors introduced usable solar cells made with silicon. Inventors continue to improve the ability of solar panels to convert sunlight into electricity.

CHAPTER FIVE

A WARMER FUTURE

The world is warming. The global temperature has risen about 1.8 degrees Fahrenheit (1 degree Celsius) since 1880. Why is Earth's energy budget shifting? Because people are increasing the amount of greenhouse gases in Earth's atmosphere. On average, the same amount of sun energy comes in every year, but less energy escapes into space.

When levels of carbon dioxide, methane, and other greenhouse gases increase, more heat is held closer to Earth.

Burning brush and other materials puts greenhouse gases into the atmosphere. Growing plants take in carbon dioxide and clean the air, but it takes a long time.

Most of these gases come from burning fossil fuels. Some are released when people clear land to grow crops or for other uses. In 2018, the atmospheric levels of carbon dioxide, a greenhouse gas, were greater than they've been in 800,000 years.

The extra energy is changing the world's climates. Warmer oceans increase the amount of moisture in the air, which can create more powerful storms. Some places receive more rain while others suffer **droughts**. Excess heat also evaporates more water from the land, making droughts worse. More heat leads to higher sea levels, which cause coastal areas to flood more easily. Warmer and longer growing seasons benefit pests such as mosquitoes and weeds. Animals and plants that can't adapt as well to the changes risk extinction.

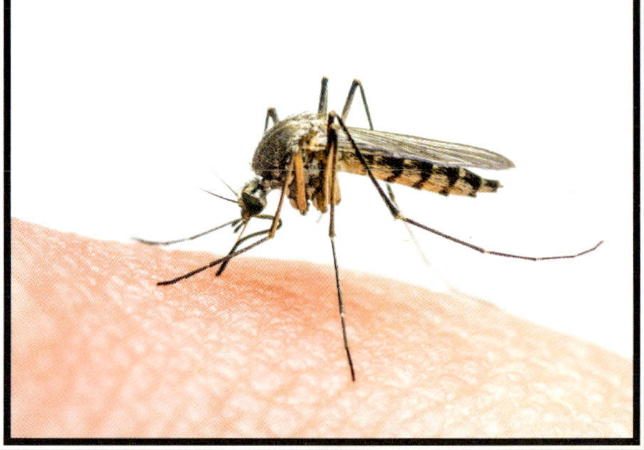

Diseases carried by mosquitoes kill more than 725,000 people each year.

A small rise in sea level makes it easier for storms to push water farther inland.

Some evidence links climate change to stronger storms, which cause more flooding.

High temperatures make droughts longer and more intense.

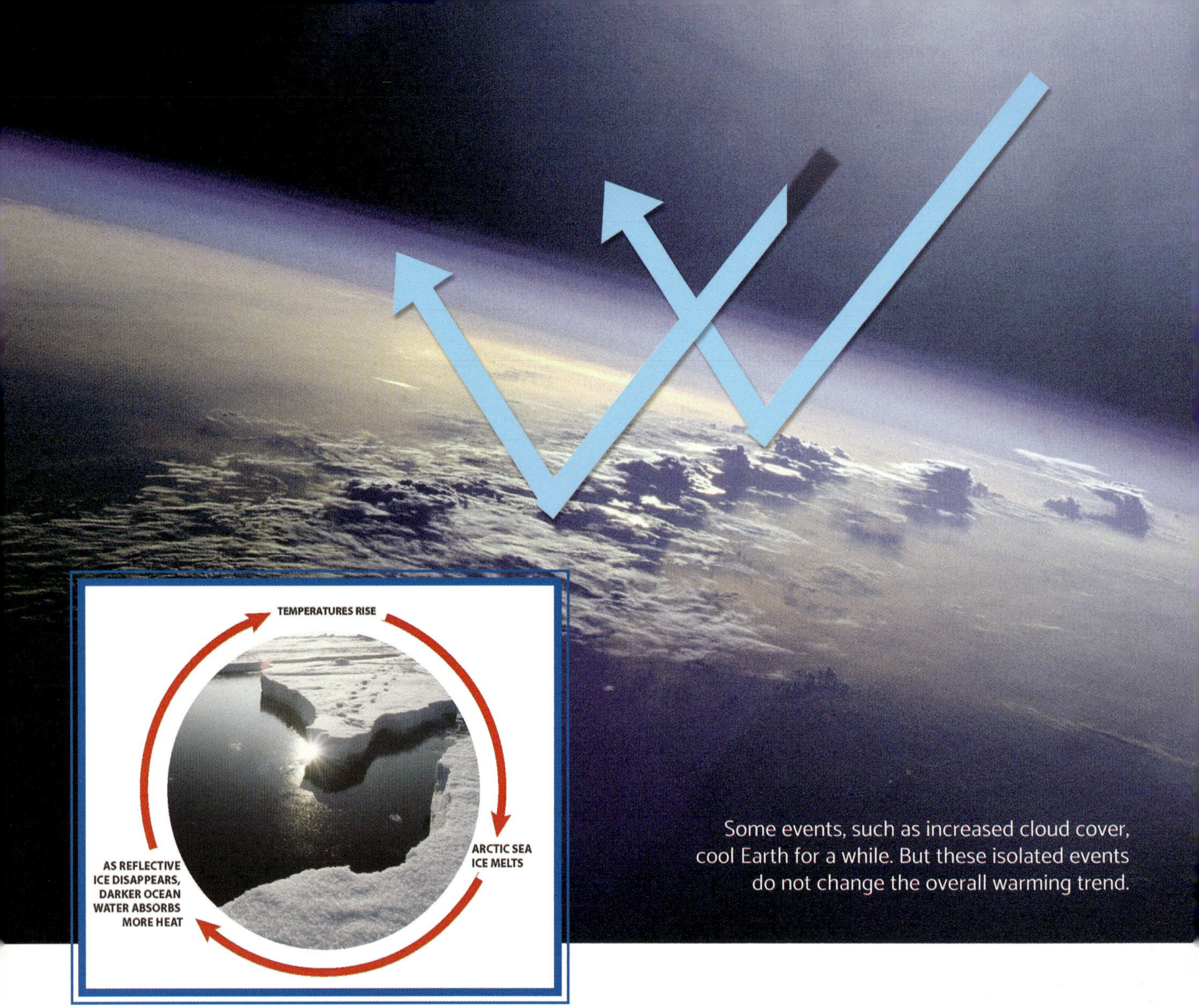

Some events, such as increased cloud cover, cool Earth for a while. But these isolated events do not change the overall warming trend.

The warming is not constant because of **feedback** loops. Some feedback loops are negative, or counter to the warming trend. Extra energy causes an event that cools the atmosphere for a time. For example, greater cloud cover due to more moisture in the air can reflect energy from the sun. Other feedback loops are positive, or in line with the warming trend. For example, the warmth melts ice and snow, which reflect sunlight, leaving bare land to absorb more energy.

High acid levels damage ocean species that use calcium carbonate to form skeletons and shells, including the corals that build reefs.

A Warming Ocean

The ocean absorbs about 90 percent of the extra heat caused by global warming. This, along with water from melting glaciers, led the global sea level to rise three inches (7.6 centimeters) from 1993 to 2017. The ocean has also absorbed large amounts of carbon dioxide, making it more acidic.

Governments and people are working to fight global warming. They're trying to reduce the use of fossil fuels and increase the use of energy sources that emit fewer greenhouse gases. Scientists are exploring ways to remove the gases that are already in the atmosphere. If people fail, the world will continue to warm, bringing even more changes to climates and ecosystems around the world. All life on Earth depends on Earth's energy budget being in balance, including us.

You can reduce, reuse, and recycle to help limit the use of fossil fuels.

Scientists are working to develop new alternatives to fossil fuels, such as fuels made from algae.

Agreement in Paris

In 2015, 195 countries adopted the Paris Agreement on climate change. They agreed to keep the global temperature from rising more than 3.6 degrees Fahrenheit (2 degrees Celsius) in this century. There is controversy about the steps that will need to be taken to honor this agreement. The world has a lot of work to do to face climate change and build a better future.

MAKE A SOLAR OVEN

Harness the sun's energy to do the work of warming food.

Important: Make sure you have an adult's permission and supervision.

Supplies

- ◊ clean pizza box
- ◊ scissors
- ◊ aluminum foil
- ◊ tape
- ◊ black paper
- ◊ plastic wrap
- ◊ a ruler
- ◊ pie plate

Directions

1. Cut a flap in the top of the pizza box, leaving an edge about two inches (five centimeters) wide.

2. Tape aluminum foil in place to cover the underside of the flap.

3. Place the black paper inside of the box to absorb heat.

4. Open the flap. Cover the gap in the top of the box by taping two layers of plastic wrap in place. One layer should be pulled tight on each side, leaving an air pocket in the middle.

5. Prop the flap open using a ruler.

6. To use your solar oven, wait for a sunny day. Choose food to warm, such as toast or s'mores. Your oven won't get hot enough to bake raw food.

7. Place your food in the pie plate and place the pie plate in the box on the black paper. Set the oven so sunlight reflects from the flap into the oven and through the plastic wrap.

8. Check after half an hour. When the food is warm, enjoy!

Glossary

absorbed (ab-ZORBD): soaked up or taken in

air pressure (air PRESH-ur): the density or weight of the air

alternatives (awl-TUR-nuh-tivs): choices different from the usual ones

atmosphere (AT-muhs-feer): the gases that surround a planet

consumers (kuhn-SOO-murs): organisms that eat or feed on other organisms

droughts (drouts): periods without sufficient rainfall or other precipitation

feedback (FEED-bak): a result of a process which then affects the process itself

friction (FRIK-shuhn): the action of one object or substance rubbing against another, which produces energy

fuels (FYOO-uhls): things used as sources of energy

fungi (FUHN-jye): plantlike organisms which can't perform photosynthesis and often grow on decaying matter

magma (MAG-muh): melted rock beneath the surface of Earth

matter (MAT-ur): material that takes up space and has weight

Index

Text-Dependent Questions

1. What are greenhouse gases and how do they affect Earth's energy budget?
2. Are humans considered carnivores, herbivores, or omnivores? Why?
3. How are fossil fuels formed?
4. What is one form of energy production that is an alternative to burning fossil fuels?
5. What is one thing people are doing to try to fight global warming?

Extension Activity

Explore a food web. Choose a habitat, such as a desert or rainforest. Research the organisms that live in the habitat. Draw a food web showing the relationship between plants, animals, and fungi. What consumes what? Show your food web to a friend and explain how energy flows through it.

About the Author

Clara MacCarald is a writer with a master's degree in ecology and natural resources. She lives with her family in an off-grid house nestled in the forests of central New York. When not parenting her daughter, she spends her time writing books about science and history for kids.

www.rourkeeducationalmedia.com

PHOTO CREDITS: Cover: highway © Surapol Usanakul / Shutterstock.com. daisies © Horum / Shutterstock.com. Pg.4-5: istock.com | Meinzahn, VAL_2016 – surfguy Pg.6-7: istock.com | monkeybusinessimages, Pg.8-9: shutterstock.com | OBprod , – shutterstock.com | u3d Pg.10-11: NASA. shutterstock.com | Nemeziya. Pg.12-13: shutterstock.com | Ziablik, shutterstock.com | Rashevskyi Viacheslav, shutterstock.com | Jon Naustdalslid, – shutterstock.com | struna. Pg.14-15: shutterstock.com | udaix, shutterstock.com | Fotos593, Shutterstock.com | Designua. Pg.16-17: shutterstock.com | Designua, shutterstock.com | LukaTDB, istock.com | ivansmuk, istock.com | ivansmuk. Pg.18-19: shutterstock.com | Rainer Fuhrmann, shutterstock.com | Pilvitus, shutterstock.com | Aphelleon. Pg.20-21: istock.com | johny87, istock.com | karlumbriaco, shutterstock.com | alinabel, istock.com | tevanovicigor. Pg.22-23: istock.com | KirsanovV , istock.com | jacobeukman, shutterstock.com | BlueRingMedia, istock.com | coffeekai. Pg.24-25: ISTOCK.COM | gsagi, istock.com | Mayerberg, istock.com | Sherron L. Pratt, istock.com | LuckyBusiness. Pg.26-27: istock.com | Gumpanat, istock.com | Zummolo, NOAA. Pg.28-29: istock.com | Vasyl Dolmatov, istock.com | egdigital, istock.com | Esteban De Armas, shutterstock.com | Ioana Catalina E. Pg.30-31: shutterstock.com | Vladyslav Trenikhin, shutterstock.com | Olivier Le Queinec, shutterstock.com | Roman Pelesh, shutterstock.com | Victor Lauer. Pg.32-33: shutterstock.com | trgrowth, istock.com | Jacek_Sopotnicki, shutterstock.com | Vecton, istock.com | ChrisVanLennepPhoto. Pg.34-34: istock.com | VanderWolf-Images, istock.com | Mimadeo, istock.com | gyn9038. Pg.36-37: istock.com | DavidSzabo, shutterstock.com | Marianna Ianovska, istock.com | Jurgute. Pg.38-39: istock.com | welcomia, shutterstock.com | Arthur Villator, istock.com | stevanovicigor, shutterstock.com | nechaevkon. Pg.40-41: NASA, istock.com | IakovKalinin, shutterstock.com | yoshi0511 | National Research Council. Pg.42-43: shutterstock.com | Kuznetcov_Konstantin, istock.com | serezniy, istock.com | Toa55. Pg.44-45: shutterstock.com | Dan Kosmayer

Edited by: Kim Thompson

Produced by Blue Door Education for Rourke Educational Media. Cover and interior design by: Jennifer Dydyk

Library of Congress PCN Data

Earth's Energy Flow / Clara MacCarald
(Science Masters)
ISBN 978-1-73161-466-7 (hard cover)
ISBN 978-1-73161-273-1 (soft cover)
ISBN 978-1-73161-571-8 (e-Book)
ISBN 978-1-73161-676-0 (e-Pub)
Library of Congress Control Number: 2019932274

Rourke Educational Media
Printed in the United States of America,
North Mankato, Minnesota